woodland rhymes for little ones

by kristy clarke

Woodland Rhymes For Little Ones
A Rhymes For Little Ones Book

dedication

Dedicated to my most favourite
little ones...
Amos, Aila, Jack, Braedon and Ben.

And to my husband Stephen
for his continued support
and encouragement.

woodland rhymes
for little ones

by kristy clarke

a winter's nut

Watch as he goes,
On tippy-toes,
To gather nuts with care.
Beneath the leaves,
Of autumn trees,
A chill upon the air.

All fattened up,
From every 'sup,
A winter coat he'll wear.
Snug in his home,
He will not roam,
Except when food is rare.

mr. Pumpernickel

Jolly Mr. Pumpernickel,
Can you come to tea?
Just follow the lane,
Up over the hill,
To the cottage by the sea.

A square of sugar for your cup?
One lump, two or three?
Oh what a lovely,
Day it is!
To have such company.

the apple bandit

My, isn't he a sneaky fellow?
Off to fetch and forage,
A little treat of something sweet,
To put into his porridge.

An apple here, a berry there,
Whatever he can find.
Nuts and seeds and even weeds.
Never does he mind.

Then at the dawn of farmer's wake,
Quick to hide his goods,
He'll throw his sack upon his back,
And scamper through the woods.

the first snow

Once upon a winter's eve,
For buds of yellow birch,
A little doe, through fallen snow,
Did wander out to search.

What magic spell has happened here?
That came without a sound.
An icy gust, of fairy dust,
Falls still upon the ground.

What wonder for the woodland fawn,
To happen on this night,
First winter's snow, she'll ever know,
To fill her heart with light.

Clementine

Sweet and sunny,
Little bunny,
Made of marshmallow fluff.
Decided to bake,
A clementine cake,
And one sugar-dusted cream puff.

Out the back door,
She hopped to the store,
For candies and sprinkles and stuff.
But when she got home,
She let out a groan,
For she'd eaten them all sure enough.

the woodland jamboree

Have you met dear Mr. Fox,
From the woodland jamboree?
No banjo star,
From near or far,
Plays better strings than he.

He'll have you on your dancing feet,
Just swinging to his banjo beat.
No cooler fox you'll ever meet,
From the woodland jamboree.

Come sing a song for Mr. Fox,
Play those spoons upon your knee.
From dusk till dawn,
The party's on!
At the woodland jamboree.

Now get up on your dancing feet,
Swing out to that banjo beat,
No cooler fox you'll ever meet,
From the woodland Jamboree.

A Rhymes For Little Ones Book
By Kristy Clarke

Kristy Clarke lives in Oakville, Ontario with her son Amos, step-son Braedon and husband Stephen. She spends her days going on many walks with Amos while dreaming up new poems and characters.

Coming soon to Rhymes For Little Ones...
Barnyard Rhymes For Little Ones By Kristy Clarke.

38160887R00015

Made in the USA
Charleston, SC
28 January 2015